AF647470

EX LIBRIS
THIS BOOK BELONGS TO:
WARNING!
DO NOT USE YOUR REAL NAME!

IF MY FATHER SAID HE WAS GOING TO COME AND TAKE ME OUT, IT WAS AS LIKELY AS NOT THAT HE WOULDN'T SHOW UP. I WOULD SAY TO THE OTHER BOYS, I HAD A WONDERFUL DAY OUT, WHEN I HAD REALLY BEEN SITTING IN A FIELD SOMEWHERE.

-DAVID CORNWELL

To my mom, who wasn't happy that the last dedication she got had only two words. This one has 22!
Love,
Mac

To my favorite humans: Katrin, Allister, and Oskar
—ML

Text copyright © 2018 by Mac Barnett • Illustrations copyright © 2018 by Mike Lowery All rights reserved. Published by Orchard Books, an imprint of Scholastic Inc., *Publishers since 1920.* ORCHARD BOOKS and design are registered trademarks of Watts Publishing Group, Ltd., used under license. SCHOLASTIC and associated logos are trademarks and/or registered trademarks of Scholastic Inc. • Game Boy is a registered trademark of Nintendo Co. Ltd. • The publisher does not have any control over and does not assume any responsibility for author or third-party websites or their content. • No part of this publication may be reproduced, stored in a retrieval system, or transmitted in any form or by any means, electronic, mechanical, photocopying, recording, or otherwise, without written permission of the publisher. For information regarding permission, write to Scholastic India Pvt. Ltd., A-27, Ground Floor, Sigma Center, Infocity-1, Sector-34, Gurgaon-122001, Haryana. • This book is a work of fiction. Names, characters, places, and incidents are either the product of the author's imagination or are used fictitiously, and any resemblance to actual persons, living or dead, business establishments, events, or locales is entirely coincidental.

ISBN 978-93-5275-774-9

The text type was set in Twentieth Century.
The display type was hand lettered by Mike Lowery.
Book design by Elizabeth Casal and Doan Buu
Published by Scholastic India Pvt. Ltd
First edition, September 2018
This reprint edition: July 2025
Printed in India at MicroPrints India, New Delhi

MAC B.
KID SPY
MAC UNDERCOVER

By **Mac Barnett**
Illustrated by **Mike Lowery**

Orchard Books
New York
An Imprint of Scholastic Inc.

ME AS A
KID
SPY!

A NOTE FROM THE AUTHOR:

FROM THE DESK OF

MAC BARNETT

MY NAME IS MAC BARNETT. I AM AN AUTHOR. BUT BEFORE I WAS AN AUTHOR, I WAS A KID. AND WHEN I WAS A KID, I WAS A SPY.

AN AUTHOR'S JOB IS TO MAKE UP STORIES. BUT THE STORY YOU ARE ABOUT TO READ IS TRUE.

THIS ACTUALLY HAPPENED TO ME.

CHAPTER 1

THE CALL

This is the house I grew up in.

It is on the top of a hill in a little town called Castro Valley. That's a real place. You can look it up.

This is really what my house looked like.

My mom and I lived there.

Since it was just the two of us, I had a lot of responsibilities: I did the dishes, packed my lunches, cooked our dinners, washed the laundry, dusted, vacuumed, and cleaned out our rabbits' litter boxes.

(I wanted a dog. We had rabbits instead.)

It was also my responsibility to answer the phone. I liked answering the phone, even though it was never for me.

One afternoon the phone rang, and it was for me.

It was the Queen of England.

"Hello?" I said.

"Hullo," she said. "Can I speak to Mac?"

"Speaking," I said.

"Mac, this is the Queen of England," she said. "I would like to ask you for a favor."

"OK," I said.

Whenever somebody asks you for a favor, it is a good idea to ask them what the favor is before you say OK.

But I had never talked to a queen before.

So I said OK.

"Wonderful," said the Queen. "I will tell you a secret. Last night, somebody stole the Crown Jewels!"

"No!" I said.

"Yes!" said the Queen. "This is the favor: You shall find the missing treasure and bring it back to me."

"Wow!" I said.

"Yes!" said the Queen.

This was very exciting.

But I had a question.

"I have a question," I said.

"I hope it is a quick question," said the Queen.

"Why me?"

The Queen of England sighed. "That is a stupid question."

"My teacher says there is no such thing as stupid questions."

The Queen of England frowned. (I could tell she was frowning, even over the phone.)

"That is just something teachers say in America. But I am not a teacher from America. I am a queen, from England."

"Oh," I said. "OK. But still. Why me? I am just a kid, and I don't even live in England."

Castro Valley is in California. You'd know that if you looked it up.

"Mac," said the Queen. "You are the smartest kid in your class. You have straight As in every subject, except handwriting."

"I'm working on that," I said.

"Then it's settled. You shall take the next flight to London."

"But tomorrow is a school day."

"I shall write a note," said the Queen.

"But my mom will be worried about me," I said.

"I shall write another note," said the Queen. "Good-bye."

She hung up.

There was a knock at the front door.

When I opened it, nobody was there.

But an envelope lay on our welcome mat.

I opened it, because I was Mac Barnett.

(I still am.)

Inside the envelope was a plane ticket and a stack of colorful British money.

It seemed like a lot of money. I couldn't tell for sure, because I wasn't British.

(I'm still not.)

I went upstairs and packed.

Like a good spy, I packed light.

I laid out some things on my bed.

My Game Boy.
Three books.
A toothbrush.
A hat.
A shirt.
A jacket.

And:

Really, they were my only blue jeans.

My mom bought me one pair at the beginning of every school year. Most kids in my school had many pairs of jeans, but my mom didn't like it when I told her that.

"Just be glad you have any jeans," she would say. "In Russia, jeans are banned."

"Banned?"

"Against the law."

"Is that true?" I would say. "That doesn't seem true."

But my mom insisted that it was true. And she only bought me one pair of jeans.

I put on my jeans, picked up my suitcase, and went downstairs.

When I was walking out the door, the phone rang.

Again.

It was the Queen of England.

Again.

"Hello?" I said.

"Hullo," she said.

"Can I speak to Mac?" she asked.

"Speaking," I said.

"I forgot to tell you one thing," said the Queen. "Be careful. This mission is extremely dangerous. Good-bye."

CHAPTER
2
SPY PLANE
ME

And that is how it happens.

One minute you are just a kid.

The next minute you are a secret agent for the Queen of England.

One night you are doing a math worksheet.

The next night you are flying on a plane to London, and you didn't even pack any math worksheets.

It takes a long time to get to London from California.

We flew through the night.

The sky outside my window was black. Out on the wing, a big jet engine roared.

I wondered how long this mission would take. It was Wednesday, and on Saturday, Derek Lafoy was having a karate birthday party. It would be nice to make it back in time for the party.

Of course, I hadn't been invited to Derek Lafoy's karate birthday party.

At least not yet. Probably because I was the only boy in my class who did not do karate for an after-school activity. Half the girls did karate too. It was the 1980s. Karate was a big deal. You can look that up.

My mom worked late, so my after-school activity was Extended Adventure After-School Day Care. There wasn't much adventure. I was the oldest one in day care by two grades. I did my homework, then played chess against little kids until my mom came to pick me up.

But! Now that I was a secret agent for the Queen of England, I figured Derek Lafoy would definitely invite me to his party.

Still, I hoped my mission didn't involve any karate. I studied my fellow passengers.

Maybe I was being followed.

(Good spies are always aware of the people around them.)

Why was the man behind me wearing sunglasses on an airplane? Was it so I couldn't see he was watching me while he pretended to read the newspaper?

What about that woman putting on perfume? Was her bottle really full of perfume? Or did it contain knockout gas?

And what about that baby? That baby had been staring at me for the past ten minutes. Was that a regular baby, or a spy baby working for the KGB?

The KGB doesn't exist anymore.
But when I was a kid, the KGB definitely existed.
The KGB was a spy agency from the Soviet Union.
The Soviet Union also doesn't exist anymore.

But back when there was a Soviet Union, the KGB meant Комите́т госуда́рственной безопа́сн ости.

That's Russian.

(They used a different alphabet in the Soviet Union. It's called the Cyrillic alphabet. You can look that up.)

In English, KGB means the "Committee for State Security," but really it means "Soviet Spies."

Stealing the Crown Jewels seemed like exactly the kind of thing the KGB would do.

Which meant that I could be flying straight into a face-off with the KGB. I was playing a dangerous game of chess against a Soviet spy. And I was much better at chess than karate.

This could be very exciting.

The man in the sunglasses snored, but it sounded like fake snoring.

The woman sprayed some more perfume, which smelled gross, like knockout gas probably does.

The baby giggled. It was a cute giggle, but also sort of menacing.

I was too excited to sleep.

So I did what I always did when I needed to quiet my brain. I took out my Game Boy, plugged in my headphones, and played SPY MASTER.

SPY MASTER was my favorite video game.

This is what the box looked like:

This is what the game looked like:

I know. I wish the graphics were better, but remember, this story takes place during my actual childhood, in the 1980s. I can't just make something easier because I wish things were different.

Still, the box gives you a pretty good idea of how fun the game was. To beat a level, you had to sneak into KGB HQ, steal some secret plans from the top floor, then parachute off the roof down into your convertible. The whole time you had to avoid getting smashed by elevators or blown up by KGB Men, who threw sticks of dynamite. It was great. I had all ten high scores.

(The best part of having a name that is three letters long is that the whole thing fits on the high-score lists of old video games.)

I was about to beat my high score when somebody tapped me on the shoulder.

It was a flight attendant.

She was pushing a big metal cart.

She smiled and said something. I couldn't hear her, because the theme song to SPY MASTER was still playing loudly in my ears.

I took off my headphones.

"Something to drink, sir?" said the flight attendant.

"A glass of milk, please," I said.

She handed me a plastic cup.

The plane hit a bump.

"Ooh!" said the flight attendant. She unlatched a tray in the seat in front of me and put the milk in a cup holder. "Be careful. You don't want to spill milk all over your jeans."

"Thanks," I said. "They're my only pair."

"Well, they're very nice," she said. "Perfectly faded."

I smiled. They were perfectly faded.

She set a plastic tray down next to my milk. "Here's your dinner."

I lifted a piece of tinfoil from the tray and found three raviolis, six green beans, and a cup of chocolate pudding.

I poked a ravioli.

"Does this have cheese in it?" I asked.

But the flight attendant was already moving down the aisle.

I ate the pudding first.

Then the ravioli.

I didn't touch the green beans.

There must have been sleeping powder in my pudding because my vision swirled and then everything went black.

There must have been cheese in the ravioli because I had really weird dreams.

There must have been a thief on the plane because when I woke up, somebody had stolen my Game Boy.

CHAPTER 3

THE TOWER

This is the Tower of London. As you can see, there is more than one tower.

"The Tower of London" is not a great name.

The Tower of London is a fortress.

The oldest tower in the Tower of London is a tall white tower, which is called the White Tower. (Good name.)

The fortress was built in 1066 by a king who conquered England, who was called William the Conqueror. (Also a good name.)

William the Conqueror built the fortress and the tower to scare English people. Since that time, the kings and queens of England have used it as a place to keep stuff:

WEAPONS,

MONEY,

PRISONERS,

ART,

A POLAR BEAR,

AN ELEPHANT,

A LION,

AND SEVERAL
OTHER KINDS
OF ANIMALS.

Henry VIII kept many of his wives, friends, and relatives at the Tower of London, before he chopped off their heads.

And for the last few centuries, the kings and queens of England have kept the Crown Jewels there too.

And so, as soon as I landed in London, I took a taxi straight to the Tower of London to search for clues.

The place was packed. Beefeaters in blue-and-red uniforms told tourists stories of treachery, violence, and love. An old man held a giant camera up to his face. Two people with purple liberty spikes kissed against an ancient wall. There were kids everywhere, kids standing near their moms and dads, kids bunched up in school groups, kids looking bored listening to music on their Walkmen. I did my best to blend in. (Good spies are invisible.)

I checked a map and made my way to a building marked "Jewel House." The Jewel House's two huge doors were closed and blocked by two huge beefeaters holding two huge battle-axes.

My mouth was dry, but I swallowed hard anyway.

"Hello," I said.

"Hullo," said the guard on the right.

"Jewel House is closed today, sonny," said the guard on the left. "The Crown Jewels is being dusted."

I knew the guard was lying to me. And I said so.

"No," I said. "There's been a robbery. I know because the Queen sent me."

The guard on the right frowned. "Clever one, isn't he?"

"Too clever," said the one on the left. "You must be the secret agent."

"I am," I said.

"Never been too fond of secret agents myself," said the guard on the right.

"I don't really like children," said the guard on the left.

The guard on the right grimaced. "And don't get me started on Americans."

I'd met plenty of people who said they didn't like children. For instance, my mom's boyfriend, Craig, said it all the time. But who didn't like secret agents?

"Wait," I said. "Secret agents are great. Why don't you like secret agents?"

"All that sneaking around, telling stories, playing tricks. Soldiering's an honest job."

"But you just lied to me right now, about the dusting," I said.

"Look at him," said the one on the left. "Clever, clever."

They uncrossed their axes and opened the doors. I stepped through the entrance and into the dark.

CHAPTER 4

QUEENLY POWER

Even though the fortress was full of towers, the Crown Jewels were kept deep below the ground. Down forty-nine steps, along a dim hallway, I walked toward the scene of the crime. It was cool and quiet underground. The only sound was the squeak of my sneakers on the stones. The hallway ended in a doorway and a sign.

I passed into a room.

There was a great glass case in the center of the floor.

The case was lined in red velvet and lit from above.

On pillows and pedestals shone treasure after treasure: scepters; crowns; diadems, which are a type of crown; daggers; tiaras (also crowns); and orbs. Everything was gold or silver and studded with gemstones that sparkled in the light. I stepped forward and gently laid a hand on the glass.

I was entranced.

I was dazzled.

But I was also confused.

"I thought she said the Crown Jewels had been stolen," I said to myself. I was alone in the room.

"Hullo," someone said, directly behind me.

CHAPTER 5
HER MAJESTY

I turned around.

It was the Queen of England.

I recognized her face right away, from the money.

The Queen of England was surrounded by twelve corgis, who nipped at one another's tails. She was wearing a purple dress and a hat of the same color. Feathers from several exotic birds poked up from the brim.

I bowed, because that seemed like something you should do when you come face-to-face with a queen.

She frowned.

I knelt, because it seemed like my bow had not been enough.

She smiled.

"Please rise," said the Queen. She held out a tin. "Would you like a biscuit?"

"A biscuit?" I said.

She shook the tin and smiled. I reached out and tried one.

The biscuit tasted like paper and dried out my mouth.

"Delicious, isn't it?" said the Queen. "Here is a fun fact: What you in America call cookies, we English call biscuits!"

"This isn't a cookie," I said. "Cookies are sweet. They have stuff that tastes good, like chocolate chips."

The Queen frowned. "Then what do you call biscuits?"

"We call them biscuits, and we feed them to dogs."

"I see," said the Queen. She put the lid on the tin and put the tin in her handbag. "How was your flight?"

"It was awful!" I said. "Somebody stole my Game Boy!"

"I don't know what that is," said the Queen.

"Oh!" I said. "It's a handheld video game console. Nintendo makes them."

"I am of the general belief that video games are rubbish," said the Queen.

"Actually, they're pretty fun!" I said. "And a lot of them really are little stories. Like Mario, he's a plumber who one day—"

"Let me give you some advice," said the Queen. "When people ask you how your flight was, they are looking for a short answer like 'good' or 'long.' They are certainly not asking to hear stories about plumbers, or misplaced Game Boys."

"It wasn't misplaced! It was stolen! Don't you think it might be related to the theft of the Crown

Jewels?" I gestured to the case full of treasures. "Also, I thought you said somebody had stolen the Crown Jewels."

"I did."

"But..."

I gestured to the case again.

"But what?"

"But...there are a bunch of jewels here."

"Mac, there are one hundred and forty objects in the Crown Jewels. They weren't all stolen."

"I see," I said.

I pulled out a notebook so I could take down a description. "So what was stolen?"

"My spoon," said the Queen.

“Your what?”

“My spoon,” said the Queen.

I started laughing.

I could tell from the Queen’s face that I shouldn’t laugh, so I stopped.

The room was quiet.

The Queen cleared her throat.

I bowed again, just to be safe.

Then I said, “Tell me more about this spoon.”

"This spoon is quite special. It is used in the coronation of kings and queens. It is called," said the Queen, "the Coronation Spoon."

"Good name," I said.

"The Coronation Spoon has been in the royal collection for more than eight hundred years."

"That's an old spoon!" I said.

"Indubitably," said the Queen. "It is made of silver and covered in gold. It is engraved with leafy scrolls and the faces of monsters. Four freshwater pearls are mounted in its stem."

I wrote this down.

"How big is it?" I asked.

"It measures ten inches."

"That's a long spoon!" I said.

"Indubitably," said the Queen.

I set down my pencil. "Look, this seems like a very nice spoon—"

"Indubitably," said the Queen.

"—but why the big fuss? It's a spoon."

"I shall tell you a story," said the Queen. "For more than one thousand years—"

"Oh boy," I said.

CHAPTER 6

KING AND QUEEN STUFF

"For more than one thousand years," said the Queen, "there has been a king or queen on the throne of England. Except for a brief interregnum."

"Interregnum?" I said.

"From the Latin," said the Queen. "You do not speak Latin?"

"I have an A in Spanish!" I said.

"Hmmm," said the Queen. "*Inter* meaning 'in between.' *Regnum* meaning 'reign.' Four hundred years ago, there was a little break between kings."

"Why?"

"England had a civil war. One side fought for King Charles I, one side was against him. Things did not end well for the king."

"What happened?"

"Regicide."

"Regicide?"

The Queen sighed.

"From the Latin. *Reg* meaning 'king.' *Cide* meaning 'kill.'"

"Regicide!" I said.

"Yes," said the Queen. "It is my least favorite type of 'cide.'"

"This is dark," I said.

"This is history," said the Queen. "King Charles I was executed. For eleven years, England had no king. A man named Oliver Cromwell named himself Lord Protector of the Commonwealth of England, Scotland, and Ireland. Cromwell hated kings. He hated queens. And he hated fun. He shut down the theaters. He outlawed pretty dresses. Instead of feasting on Christmas, people fasted. If Game Boys had been invented, he would have taken those away too. A terrible man."

"But you just said video games are rubbish."

"There is a considerable difference between believing something is rubbish and believing it should not exist," said the Queen. "Remember that."

I never forgot it.

"It was like the whole country got grounded," I said.

AND MAJOR PARTY POOPER!

SOME of THE STUFF CROMWELL HATED:

"Indeed," said the Queen. "Times were grim. For money, Cromwell melted the Crown Jewels. He sold off the gold, the silver, the gems to fill his own coffers. Every crown, every scepter, every sword was destroyed. Only one thing survived."

"The spoon," I said.

"The spoon," said the Queen. "When King Charles II returned to the English throne, he ordered his goldsmiths and jewelers to remake the lost treasures. Some of those replicas stand behind you right now. And King Charles II tracked down the spoon, and when he was crowned, a bishop used it to pour oil on his hand."

"What?"

"King and queen stuff," said the Queen.

"OK," I said.

"You asked why this spoon is so valuable," said the Queen. "What do people want more than anything else? Tradition. This spoon may be only ten inches long, but it reaches all the way to England's misty past, through times that were dark, and times that were glorious, and my goodness your handwriting is terrible."

I'd been writing all this down, and the Queen was now looking over my shoulder.

"I'm working on that!" I said.

"As you should be. What does that say?"

"It says 'glorious.'"

"I can't tell if that's a 'g' or a 'q.' You need to put the little curve on the bottom of your stems."

"My mom always tells me that too," I said.

"She is right."

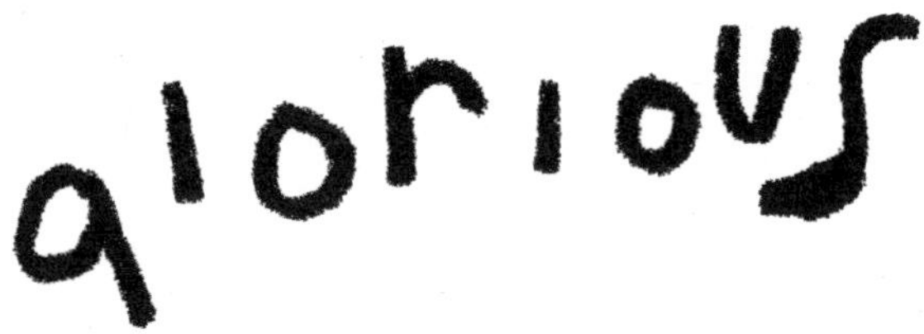

"OK," I said. "Well, I'm going to search this place for clues."

"There is no need," said the Queen. "I already know who took my spoon."

"You do?"

"Yes."

"Was it the KGB?"

"The KGB?" said the Queen.

This seemed exactly like something the KGB would do.

"No. It was not the KGB. It was the President of France. He left a note."

The Queen reached into her handbag and took out an envelope. She handed it to me, and I opened it.

"Wow," I said. "The President of France has terrible handwriting too! Some of these letters are backward!"

"So what?" said the Queen.

"So, even if I do have terrible handwriting, I could grow up to be president!"

"Yes," said the Queen. "Of France."

"What's that supposed to mean?" I asked.

"Just read the letter," said the Queen.

"You stuck your tongue out at the President of France?" I said.

DEAR YOUR MAJESTY,

I SNUCK INTO the TOWER OF LONDON and STOLE YOUR SPOON. NOW YOU WILL NEVER GET IT BACK. This WILL TEACH YOU NOT to STICK OUT YOUR TONGUE AT ME NEXT time WE HAVE LUNCH.

HA HA,

the president of FRANCE

"I thought his back was turned!" said the Queen.

"Hmmm," I said.

"He was being rude!" she said.

"OK . . . ," I said.

"In any case," said the Queen, "I want you to take the hovercraft to France tonight and fetch my spoon."

"OK," I said. "Do I get any spy gear?"

"Spy gear?" asked the Queen.

"Yeah," I said. "Like James Bond."

The Queen sniffed.

"Mac, James Bond is a made-up character in a made-up story. This is totally real life."

"Oh," I said. "Right."

"Of course you get spy gear," said the Queen.

She reached into her giant handbag and removed a pair of what looked like ordinary sunglasses.

"These may look like ordinary sunglasses, but they are in fact night-vision spectacles. Wear them and you can see in the dark."

"But won't I look funny wearing sunglasses at night?" I said.

"Not if you have confidence!" said the Queen. "Confidence!"

She reached into her handbag again and pulled out a box.

"This is a secret identity kit. You won't be able to check into a hotel or drive a car if people think you're a kid."

I opened the box.

"Your name is Hugh Anthony Cregg III, and you are a piano tuner from Kalamazoo, Michigan. Got that?"

"But aren't I a little short to be an adult?"

"Yes." The Queen frowned. "I did expect you to be taller."

"I'm the shortest boy in my class," I said.

"Well," said the Queen. "Confidence! People probably won't ask you about your height. It's rude."

"OK," I said.

"Of course," said the Queen, "there are a lot of rude people in France. On the other hand, there are a lot of short people in France, so you should be all right."

"Hmmm," I said.

"Here is a top secret report on the President of France. It may contain information vital to your mission."

"But most of the words are blacked out."

"Yes. It's redacted. The best information is always blacked out of top secret reports. It's top secret."

"But this is unreadable," I said.

"Finally," said the Queen, "I will loan you one of my dogs to take on your mission. You may select your favorite. Corgis, line up!"

The Queen's dogs stopped nipping one another's tails and arranged themselves into a tidy line, shoulder to shoulder. I studied them carefully.

"Are these dogs trained assassins?" I asked.

"Of course not!" said the Queen. "How dreadful."

"Are they robots?" I asked.

"Don't be ridiculous," said the Queen.

"Then why are you giving me one?"

"Loaning you one," said the Queen. "The life of a spy is lonely. It's nice to have company."

I pointed at a little dog on the end.

"That one," I said.

"Freddie?" said the Queen. "But Freddie is a runt."

"That's what everybody calls me at school!" I said.

"Freddie?" said the Queen.

"No! Runt!" I said.

"Ah," said the Queen.

She picked up Freddie and placed him in my arms. He began licking my face.

"No licking, Freddie," said the Queen.

Freddie kept licking.

"Well," said the Queen. "You'd better get going. The hovercraft leaves soon."

Freddie and I walked to the door. But I had one more question.

"Just one more question," I said.

"Oh, for goodness' sake," said the Queen.

"How long do you think this mission will take?" I asked.

"It will take as long as it takes," said the Queen. "Why?"

"It's just that this weekend Derek Lafoy is having a karate birthday party."

The Queen gave me a serious look. "And were you invited to Derek Lafoy's karate birthday party?" she asked.

"No, but—"

"Good luck on your mission," said the Queen.

HAPPY
EVERYBODY WAS KUNG FU FIGHTING
BIRTHDAY

CHAPTER 7

A THREAT

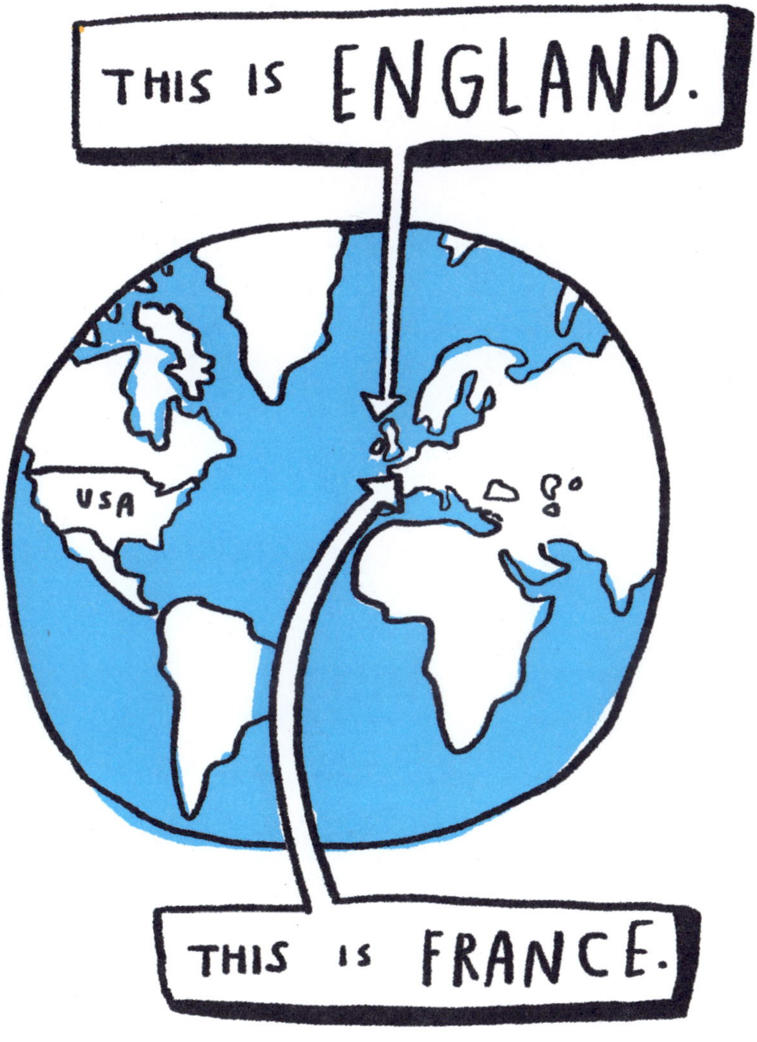
THIS IS ENGLAND.
USA
THIS IS FRANCE.

The channel of water in the middle of England and France is called the English Channel. (Good name, if you're English.)

In 1066, William the Conqueror crossed the channel in a boat to take England's crown.

In 1989, I crossed the channel in a hovercraft so I could take back England's spoon.

In case you couldn't tell, that's me at the front of the hovercraft, in disguise.

In this picture I am thinking: How can I get the President of France to give me back the Queen's spoon?

The salty air blew through my mustache.

Seagulls cried.

Freddie licked my ankle.

By the time we reached France, I still had not thought up a plan.

We took the train into Paris, where the President of France lives.

I checked into a fancy hotel, using the name Hugh Anthony Cregg III.

"And what is your dog's name, monsieur?" asked the woman at the hotel desk.

(*Monsieur* means "sir" in French. You can look it up. That, like the rest of the stuff in this book, is true.)

"His name is Rockford," I said, because Freddie looked like he might enjoy having a secret identity too.

In a grand room overlooking a river, Freddie and I sat on a bed with many pillows.

Some way, somehow, I had to get that spoon back.

"Got any ideas, Freddie?" I asked.

Freddie's stomach growled.

Then he licked a pillow.

I picked up the phone and ordered room service.

Ten minutes later a man arrived with two silver trays.

(One for me, one for Freddie.)

Five minutes after that, the phone rang.

It was the Queen of England.

"Hello?" I said.

"Hullo," she said. "May I please speak to Mac?"

"Speaking," I said.

"Wrong," said the Queen. "You are traveling as Hugh Anthony Cregg III. Remember that."

"OK," I said.

"Now," said the Queen, "what are you doing?"

"I'm eating a cheeseburger," I said.

"Me too!" said the Queen. "Have you found my spoon?"

"Well," I said, "not yet."

"Mac," said the Queen.

"Hugh," I said.

"Hugh," said the Queen, "I am not paying you to sit around eating cheeseburgers."

"You're not paying me at all," I said.

"That's beside the point," said the Queen. "You are my secret agent! Get to work!"

The line went dead.

I ate a French fry.

The phone rang again.

"Hello, Your Majesty," I said. "Hugh speaking."

"Mac." The voice on the other line was muffled and deep. "Forget about the spoon. Go home."

"Who is this?" I asked.

"Abandon this mission if you ever want to see your Game Boy again!"

The line went dead.

By now my fries were cold.

I gave my plate to Freddie to lick.

So the President of France had stolen my Game Boy too.

I knew one thing for sure: I knew my mom was never going to buy me another Game Boy. She'd saved up for it. It was my Big Birthday Gift.

I knew another thing for sure: I knew how I was going to get the Queen's spoon back from the President of France.

CHAPTER 8

OH AND ALSO

One more related thing I knew for sure: I also knew how I was going to get my Game Boy back from the President of France.

CHAPTER 9

MY SECRET PLAN

If the President of France thought he could go around taking stuff, I would have to speak the only language he would understand. No, not French. I didn't know French. I am talking about the language of taking stuff.

Here was my plan: Since the President of France had taken something precious from the Queen (her priceless spoon) and from me (my brand-new Game Boy), I would take something precious from France.

And then I would make a trade.

Maybe you're thinking this is stealing.

Well, it's not.

Remember: My plan was to take something and then trade it back.

That is more like borrowing.

Maybe you're thinking that borrowing involves asking for permission.

OK. You have a point.

But if you want stories of pure do-goodery, I suggest you read a different type of story, like *Great Deeds of the Founding Fathers*, or *Kids Open a Rescue Shelter for Owls*. This is a Secret Agent Story. And in the next chapter, I am going to break into a museum and steal a priceless work of art.

KIDS OPEN A
RESCUE SHELTER
FOR OWLS
BY
GREAT DEEDS OF THE FOUNDING FATHERS
AWESOME ABE!
AND MANY OTHERS!

CHAPTER
10
ART
HEIST

This is the Louvre.

It is one of the greatest museums in the world.
Inside you will find many priceless works of art.

The Seated Scribe
(Good name.)

The Lion with an Articulated Tail
(Good name.)

And this portrait of a woman named Lisa, which might be the most famous painting in the world.

It's called the Mona Lisa.

(Good name.)

Even the building itself is a work of art, one that people have been working on for more than four hundred years.

In the 1500s, the King of France built this:

In the 1800s, the Emperor of France added this:

And in the 1980s, the President of France hired a man called I. M. Pei to add this:

Today, most people love Pei's pyramid. But when I was a kid, many people hated it. They thought a sleek glass shape looked silly next to all those old buildings. They thought it was too modern. They thought it was too new. They thought the President of France had built a monument to himself, like a pharaoh of Egypt.

But I thought the pyramid was great. (I still do.) I thought it was great because I was a kid, and most kids like new things, because kids are new things too.

I also thought it was great because I was a secret agent, and most secret agents like glass things, because glass is easy to break into.

And so, late one night in 1989, I found myself perched on the side of I. M. Pei's great glass pyramid, dressed in black, wearing sunglasses, with Freddie strapped to my back.

Here is a step-by-step guide to breaking into the Louvre.

Kids, you should not do this in real life.

But I did. And here's how.

A STEP-BY-STEP GUIDE TO BREAKING INTO THE LOUVRE

STEP ONE: I placed a bath mat I'd taken from the hotel tub on a pane of glass, suction cups down.

1

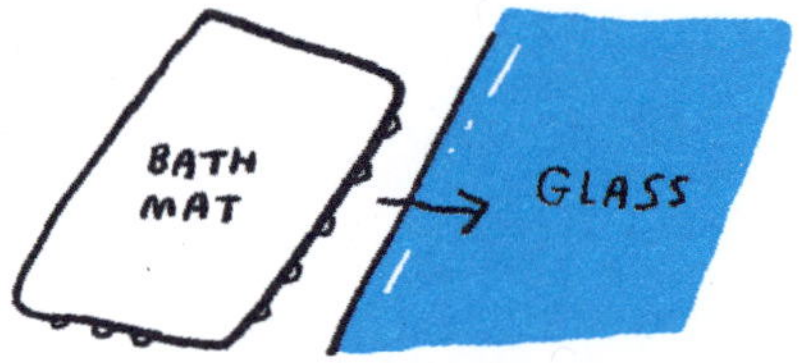

STEP TWO: I pried a diamond off Freddie's collar.

2

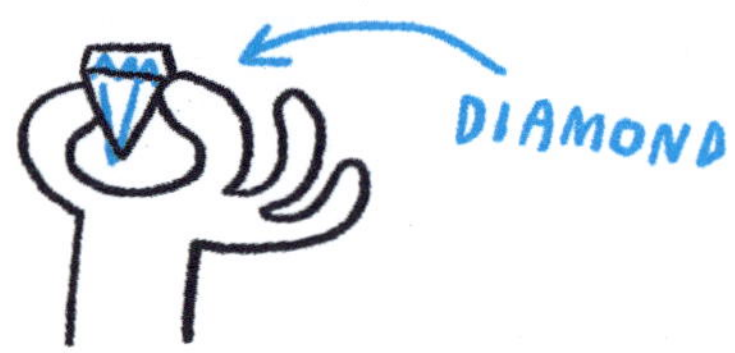

STEP THREE: I said, "Thanks, Freddie." Freddie licked my neck.

3

STEP FOUR: Very carefully, I used the diamond to cut a large rectangular shape around the bath mat.

4

STEP FIVE: I lifted the bath mat and a piece of glass with it. I said, "We're in, Freddie." He licked my neck again.

STEP SIX: Using a rope made from sheets I'd also taken from the hotel, I lowered myself into the museum.

7 STEP SEVEN: Now here's where things get interesting. Freddie and I down a flight of steps.

the guard house and

sleeping

kind of like a Tyrannosaurus rex.

using seven bananas, which is

why secret agents should carry bananas with them at all times.

cut the red wire or the blue wire? Easy: I cut all the wires.

disabled the alarm

seven-digit code, which was (and still is)

a ham sandwich. Then all there was to it was to

and there we were. Standing in front of the Mona Lisa.

"We did it, Freddie," I said, and tried to wipe the mustard from the sandwich off my shirt.

CHAPTER II

TO ROB A THIEF

The Mona Lisa was smaller than I thought it would be. It was also greener than I thought it would be, but that's probably just because I was wearing night-vision sunglasses.

Very carefully, I lifted the painting off the wall.

I paused, holding the painting aloft, bracing for an alarm.

After five seconds of silence, I smiled.

"Looks like step seven worked," I said to Freddie, who was busy licking the mustard off my shirt.

I tucked the Mona Lisa under my arm and made for the exit.

"Halt!" someone cried in the dark.

I froze.

"Turn around!"

I turned around.

I was face-to-face with a guard.

"Hands in the air!" the guard shouted.

"But then I'll drop the Mona Lisa," I said.

"Good point," said the guard. "Hand me the painting."

Reluctantly, I gave the guard the Mona Lisa.

He pulled out a pair of handcuffs and chained me to the handrail of a nearby staircase.

I slumped against the wall.

"Be careful where you sit," said the guard. "That spot is dusty. You don't want to get those jeans dirty."

How could I worry about my jeans at a time like this, when my whole mission was falling apart?

Still, they *were* great jeans. I shifted to a clean spot.

"This is all a mistake," I said. "My name is Hugh Anthony Cregg III, and I am simply here from Kalamazoo, Michigan, to tune the Louvre's pianos."

The guard laughed.

"Wait here, Mr. Cregg. We'll—"

"Mr. Cregg III," I said.

"Wait here, Mr. Cregg III. Soon you'll be tuning all the pianos you want—in jail."

"Huh?" I said.

But the guard was already gone.

CHAPTER 12

CAPTURED

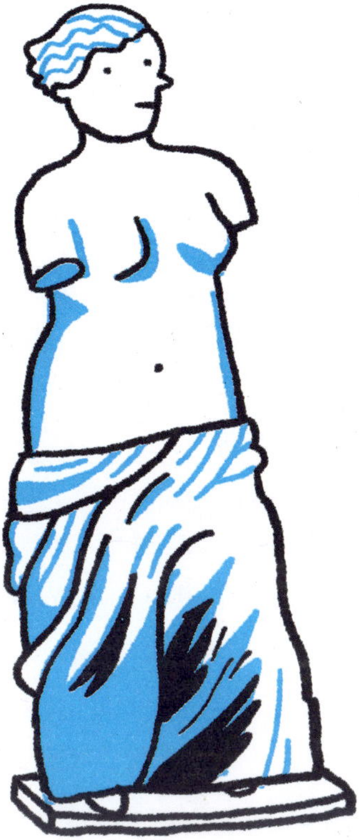

I expected to be arrested immediately.

I sat handcuffed to the rail for hours.

Luckily, I had a nice view: I was directly across from the Venus de Milo. (That name means "Venus of Milos." Milos is the name of the island where the statue was discovered, but nobody knows for sure if it is supposed to be Venus. Pretty good name, six out of ten.)

Staring at the statue gave me an idea.

"Freddie!" I said. "I need you to chew off my right arm!"

Freddie stared at me.

"It's our only hope at escape! Do it now!"

Freddie got up on his hind legs and licked my wrist.

"Well," I said, "it's a start."

But before I could train Freddie to free me from my bonds, an alarm blared.

Another guard appeared.

She rushed to where I sat on the ground.

"Monsieur!" she said, followed by a bunch of French.

(I didn't speak French.)

When she figured out I spoke English, she said, "Are you all right?"

"Yes," I said.

"The Mona Lisa is missing!" she said. "Did you see the robbery?"

"See the robbery?" I said. "I *did* the robbery."

She seemed surprised. I figured I should come clean. When my mom caught me doing something bad, it was always best to confess everything. I got in less trouble that way.

"Surely you are joking, monsieur," she said. "And you are not very funny."

"I am not joking," I said. "And actually a lot of people in my class think that I am pretty funny."

"Your class?"

I remembered my disguise.

"My class . . . ical music appreciation group. I am a piano tuner from Kalamazoo, Michig—"

"I do not care," said the guard. "If you stole the Mona Lisa, where is it, and why are you handcuffed to this staircase?"

"I already gave it back," I said. "I handed it to the other guard."

"The other guard?"

"Yeah," I said. "He had light hair, serious eyes, and a sad smile. Oh, and green skin, but that was probably just my night-vision sunglasses."

"Monsieur," said the guard, "there is no guard here by that description."

"Then who did I give the Mona Lisa to?" I asked.

The guard pulled out a walkie-talkie.

"Perhaps you should talk to the President of France," she said.

POLICE SUSPECT SKETCH
LIGHT HAIR
SERIOUS EYES
SAD SMILE

CHAPTER 13

RENDEZVOUS

This is the Arc de Triomphe.

On a foggy night, I met there with the President of France.

Its name means "Arch of Triumph." As you can see, it is an arch. It was built by the Emperor of France to celebrate triumph.

Sure, good name. But on that night I did not feel triumphant. I was utterly defeated.

The President of France looked very disappointed in me.

Later, when I saw pictures of him, I realized that he always looked disappointed.

At the time, it was hard not to take it personally. He wore a thick coat and pulled it around himself.

"It's cold out here," I said.

"*Oui*," said the President of France.

(I knew what that meant.)

"Maybe we should meet somewhere warm?" I said. "Like your palace?"

"I take it you are a secret agent," said the President of France.

"*Oui*," I said.

"Then this is how we must meet. In the night. In the fog. In the cold."

"OK," I said. "Mr. President, the world is a mess, and I think it is all my fault."

"I am sure you are being hard on yourself," he said. "Tell me everything."

I told him everything.

"You are right," said the President. "This is all your fault."

I frowned. "Well, it's a little bit your fault too. For stealing the Coronation Spoon. And my Game Boy."

"But I did not steal the spoon. Or your Game Boy. I already own a Game Boy."

"You do? Do you play SPY MASTER?"

"*Oui.*"

"What's your high score?"

"Four thousand."

"Pretty good," I said.

(Mine was way higher.)

"I will tell you," said the President of France, "I am very happy to meet another grown man who plays a Game Boy."

"Actually, I am just a kid."

"Ah," said the President of France. He looked even more disappointed. "You did seem very short. But then, so was the man who built this arch."

(He was right. You can look that up.)

"I think it's cool you play Game Boy," I said. "My mom's boyfriend, Craig, never plays Nintendo with me. He says video games are immature, and that boys go outside and wrestle."

"Wrestle?" said the President of France.

"Yeah. He says he's going to teach me wrestling moves, but then he just pins me to the ground and laughs. I don't know what he's trying to prove. He's a grown-up. I'm a kid."

"Sounds like it is Craig who is immature."

"Yeah!" I high-fived the President of France.

"Tell me," he said. "Why does the Queen of England think that I stole her spoon?"

"She thinks you're mad at her because when you had lunch, she stuck her tongue out at you."

The President was astonished.

"She stuck her tongue out at me?"

"Yeah," I said.

"I must have had my back turned," said the President. "I had no idea."

He looked very sad.

I was starting to believe he was innocent.

But what about the note?

"But what about the note?" I said.

"What note?"

I showed him the letter from the Tower of London.

The President shook his head.

"But this is not my handwriting. It is awful! The 'R's are not even facing the right way!"

"The 'N's aren't either," I said.

"Well, this is obviously a fake. I have wonderful handwriting."

"You do?"

"Of course. I am the President of France."

"Well, now I don't know what to do," I said.

"It is obvious," said the President. "You must retrieve the Mona Lisa. She is priceless."

I'd been wondering something.

"Why is the Mona Lisa so valuable?" I asked. "It's not even very big."

"It is her smile," said the President. "Why does she smile so? What does she know? Many have guessed. Nobody knows for sure. The Mona Lisa is a mystery. And what do people want more than anything else? Mystery. To possess the unknowable."

"The Queen of England says more than anything else people want—"

"Do not speak to me of the Queen," said the President of France. "You must go now!"

"But why would you trust me?" I said. "I ruined everything."

"And that is why you must fix everything," said the President. "You are a secret agent. That is your job."

"Not anymore," I said. "I quit."

CHAPTER 14

RAIN IN THE DARK

It began to rain.

I walked along the river.

When you are feeling sad, it is wonderful to walk alone in Paris, along the river, in the rain.

But I was not walking alone.

I was walking with Freddie, who was wagging his tail and licking everything.

"Stop it, Freddie!" I said. "You're ruining the mood!"

But Freddie didn't stop. At this point it should be clear that Freddie didn't listen to anybody.

I tried to block out Freddie and sink into my sadness.

How much money was left in my envelope?

Was it enough to buy a plane ticket home?

Could I make it back in time for Derek Lafoy's karate birthday party?

Did it even matter, since I hadn't been invited?

"Does any of it matter?" I asked Freddie, who was licking a cobblestone.

Nearby, in a phone booth, a telephone rang.

It was the middle of the night.

Nobody was around.

The phone rang and rang.

I walked over and picked it up.

It was for me.

"Hullo," said the Queen.

"Hello," I said.

There was an unpleasant crunching sound on the line.

"Please excuse my crunching," said the Queen. "I'm just having some biscuits before bedtime. How is it going with the spoon?"

"Awful," I said. "The President of France didn't take it."

"He didn't?"

"No. He didn't even know you stuck your tongue out at him."

"Oh," said the Queen. "Well, I hope you didn't tell him."

"I did," I said.

"Oh dear," said the Queen.

"Anyway," I said, "I quit."

"Well," said the Queen, "I can see why."

"You're not going to ask me to finish the case?"

"No," said the Queen. "Why would I?"

"Is this some mind game?" I asked. "Are you trying to trick me into staying on the case?"

"Not at all," said the Queen. "You've done nothing so far but muck things up."

"Well, you haven't exactly helped!" I said. "You sent me to the President of France!"

"He left a note!" said the Queen.

"He didn't write it!" I said.

"Then who did?"

I dropped the phone.

It dangled from its cord.

(It was the 1980s. Phones had cords. You can look that up.)

I pulled the note out of my pocket and picked the phone back up.

"Who wrote that note?" I said.

"That's what I just asked you," said the Queen.

"Whoever wrote it must have known that you stuck your tongue out at the President of France. Whoever wrote it must have been at that lunch."

"Listen, Mac," said the Queen, "if you are insinuating that I stole my own spoon—"

"Was there anyone else at that lunch?"

"What?"

"Was anybody else at lunch with you that day?"

The line was quiet while the Queen thought.

"Well, let's see... There was me... and the President of France."

I rolled my eyes.

"Are you rolling your eyes?" asked the Queen.

"Yes," I said.

"Well, stop. Picturing you over there in France, rolling your eyes, is ruining my concentration. Now, where was I? Ah! Yes. The lunch. It was me... and the President of France... and a young man with light hair, and serious eyes, and a sad smile... I believe he was an officer from the KGB."

"THE KGB!"

"There's no use shouting," said the Queen. "Nineteen eighties pay phone technology is perfectly adequate for—"

I stopped listening.

Of course it was the KGB.

The backward letters in the note were Cyrillic.

The KGB Man had disguised himself as a museum guard.

And, come to think of it, as the flight attendant.

I'd been followed this whole time by a secret agent of the KGB, and I'd been one-upped again and again!

Well, it was time to turn the tables.

I hung up on the Queen of England and caught a plane to Moscow.

HE WAS EVERYWHERE!

CHAPTER
15
KGB HQ

This is Lubyanka Square.

It is home to two famous buildings.

One of these buildings is the headquarters of a giant Russian toy store called Detsky Mir. *Detsky Mir* means "Kids' World."

Cool name.

The other building is called the Lubyanka.

It was the headquarters of the KGB.

The biggest toy store in Europe sat directly across from a command center for spies.

(It still does. You can look that up.)

This building on the left is full of toys.

This building on the right is full of spies.

Where would you rather go?

I sighed, and went right.

With Freddie in my arms, I burst through the front doors of KGB headquarters.

A spy sat at a desk.

"I demand to see, um," I said. "Uh. I don't know his name. He's a KGB Man."

"We've been expecting you," said the spy behind the desk. "Come right in."

I was shown to an office and asked to wait.

"He will be here shortly," said the spy. "He is just getting in from Paris, and his flight was delayed."

"OK," I said.

The walls of the office were pale green and lined with wooden bookshelves. There was a handsome desk with a phone, a lamp, and a hand-carved chess set. There was a bowl of chocolates too. A large window looked out onto a snowy square. It was nice.

The office door opened and the KGB Man entered, carrying a suitcase. I recognized him from the plane and the Louvre, although he was now dressed in a drab and severe KGB uniform. He smiled sadly when he saw me.

"Ah!" he said. "You beat me here. Very good. Very good. And I see you helped yourself to those chocolates."

I blushed.

The KGB Man was already gaining the upper hand. I had to take control!

I rose from my chair. "I'm here for the spoon!"

"Please," said the KGB Man. "Sit down and we can discuss this like secret agents."

The KGB Man sat at his desk and spoke some Russian into a phone.

There was a knock on the door, and someone delivered a silver tray.

"Coffee?" the KGB Man asked.

"I don't drink coffee," I said. "I'm a kid."

"Of course," said the KGB Man. "Perhaps some milk, then?"

"Well," I said, "I do like milk."

The KGB Man poured himself some coffee from a tall and shiny pot.

Then he lifted a silver pitcher and poured me a cup of milk. The cup was blue and white, and decorated with tiny complicated patterns. I'd never drunk milk from a cup so beautiful.

The KGB Man splashed some milk into his coffee and took a spoon from the breast pocket of his coat, which he used to slowly stir his drink.

The spoon was gold, etched with leaves and the faces of monsters. Four pearls were set in its handle.

I stood up again.

"The Coronation Spoon!"

The KGB Man looked down and shrugged.

"Ah!" he said. "This spoon? It is a souvenir. I picked it up in England."

He laid it down on the tray.

The KGB Man opened his suitcase and took out my Game Boy and the Mona Lisa.

"Yes," he said, "I found some wonderful souvenirs on my trip."

"You fiend!" I cried. "Why are you taking all this stuff? And why are you showing it all to me?"

"Why indeed," said the KGB Man. "It is not

for you to understand why. You are a spy. Secret agents are like children. They do what they are told. You hear your mother and Craig arguing late one night. The next morning they tell you that you are going to summer camp. You may ask why, and your mother may answer, but that does not mean you will understand."

"Wait," I said. "That happened to me. How do you know that happened to me?"

The KGB Man shrugged. "I am KGB."

He pointed to his desk.

"The world is a chessboard. Secret agents, they are merely pieces, moving in little patterns across the squares. Powerless."

"But you're a secret agent," I said.

"For now." He picked up a pawn and twirled it between his fingers. "Tell me. Who is the most powerful in the game of chess?"

"The queen!" I said. "She goes wherever she wants to!"

"But she is stuck on the board," said the KGB Man. "No. It is not the queen. It is the player. The one who moves the pieces."

"Oh," I said. "OK."

"Today I am a spy," said the KGB Man. "But I will not be forever. I have plans."

He set the pawn down on the board and smiled at me.

"You want this stuff back? I will give you a chance. You and I, we will have a competition."

"Deal!" I said.

I reached for a white pawn. It is a lot easier to win at chess if you make the first move.

"Not chess," he said. "Karate."

The KGB Man tore off his uniform. Underneath, he was wearing a white gi and a black belt.

At this point it should be clear that I did not know karate.

"Hi-yah!" shouted the KGB Man.

He leapt across the desk and set upon me with furious chops and punches.

Books were knocked everywhere. The chess set was toppled to the floor. Freddie began barking furiously and wagging his tail.

For a time I was able to hide underneath the desk.

I flashed back to everything I knew about karate from listening to kids talk in the schoolyard. Derek Lafoy was always going on about pressure points. He said the human body had seven of them, and a single hit to one could knock someone out, or even kill them. Often he would demonstrate by aiming a slow-motion chop at the crook of my neck. "I won't actually do it," he would always say. "Otherwise I'd go to jail."

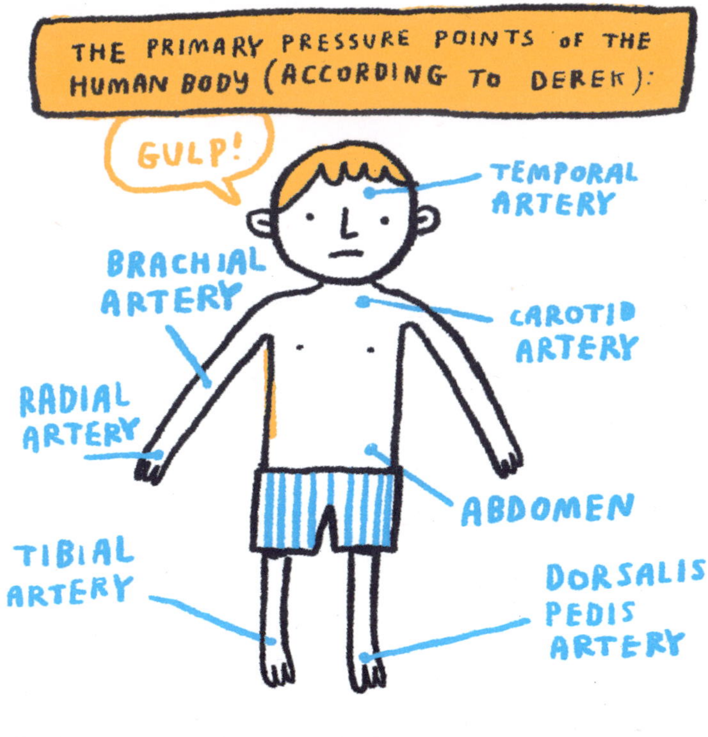

Pressure points. They were my only hope.

"Hi-yah!" I cried. I rushed out from beneath the desk and attempted to land a chop to the KGB Man's neck.

The KGB Man swept my legs and I fell to the ground.

"Give up?" he asked.

"Never!"

He twisted my arm behind my back and pushed my face into the carpet.

It was a beautiful rug.

"Give up?"

"No," I said. My defiant answer was muffled somewhat by the carpet.

The KGB Man placed me in a vicious headlock. His bicep was lodged against my windpipe. I could hardly breathe.

"Freddie!" I cried. "Help! Attack!"

Freddie was in the corner, joyfully licking some spilled milk.

I rolled my eyes.

Then I got an idea.

I tucked my chin into the crook of the KGB Man's elbow and licked it.

"Ew!" The KGB Man leapt up and wiped his arm off on his gi.

I rose to my feet and assumed a tough karate pose.

"Did you just lick my arm?" the KGB Man asked.

"Yeah!" I said.

I nodded at Freddie, who seemed to be wagging at me admiringly.

"Hmmm," said the KGB Man. "OK. That is enough karate."

He picked up his chair and sat back down at his desk. With a fancy tea towel, he wiped my spit off his arm.

"I won!" I said.

The KGB Man shook his head. "No. You did not win."

"OK," I said. "Then let's call it a draw."

"No," said the KGB Man. "You were very much outmatched. But you did not give up. I admire your spirit. And so I will offer you a trade. Please, sit down."

I did.

"What do I want with this spoon? I have plenty of spoons. What do I want with this painting? It does not go with the decor of my house. What do I want with this Game Boy? I have already beaten the game SPY MASTER."

"You beat it?" I said.

"Yes. First try. It is an OK game. Pretty fun. But why do the bad guys have to be KGB Men?"

"That's how it always is," I said.

"Not in the Soviet Union," said the KGB Man. "In any case, I will trade you all these things for something much more valuable. Your American blue jeans."

"What?" I said.

"Da," said the KGB Man.

"What does that mean?"

"Yes."

"But why would you want my blue jeans?"

"I will tell you a story," said the KGB Man. "In 1898—"

"Oh boy," I said.

"In 1898," said the KGB Man, "the building we are sitting in now was built. It was the offices of the All-Russia Insurance Company, which was a giant company that sold insurance in all of Russia."

"Good name," I said.

"*Da,*" said the KGB Man. "But in 1917, there was a revolution. The emperor of Russia was executed—"

"Regicide?" I said.

"I do not know this word," said the KGB Man.

"It's from the Latin," I said.

"The Emperor of Russia was replaced with the Chairman of the Council of People's Commissars of the Soviet Union."

"Long name," I said.

"They got rid of the eagles on flags and replaced them with hammers and sickles."

"And in this building, they got rid of the All-Russia Insurance Company and replaced it with the All-Russian Extraordinary Commission for Combating Counter-Revolution and Sabotage."

"Really long name," I said.

"Too long," said the KGB Man. "So the All-Russian Extraordinary Commission for Combating Counter-Revolution and Sabotage started calling itself the Cheka. Then the Cheka started calling itself the GPU. The GPU started calling itself the OGPU. Then the OGPU started calling itself the NKVD. Finally, the NKVD started calling itself the KGB. Who knows? Maybe one day, we change our name again. All these names, they mean the same thing: secret agents."

"But what does this have to do with jeans?" I asked.

"After the revolution, everything was different. No emperor. No eagles. No insurance companies. And no jeans. In the Soviet Union, American blue jeans are banned."

"Banned?"

"Against the law."

So it was true.

The KGB Man gazed sadly at his pale green walls.

"When I was a child, I caught jeans fever. I saw a picture in a magazine, a boy and a girl in America. They were dancing, in a basement, wearing their blue jeans. They were so happy. Their jeans were so perfectly faded. I wanted a pair."

For a single moment, the KGB Man seemed to be just a KGB Boy, begging his mother for some back-to-school jeans.

But he slammed his fist against the desk.

"Russian jeans, they are no good!" said the KGB Man. "They do not fade. I have tried to boil them, run them over with a motorcycle, tie them in knots and throw them in the river. No good."

"But you travel around the world," I said. "Why don't you just buy some American blue jeans and bring them back?"

The KGB Man shook his head.

"That is a crime. Jean crime. For smuggling blue jeans, a Russian would lose their job, go to jail. That is why I needed you, an American, to wear your jeans here."

"Wait," I said. "This whole thing, the spoon, the Mona Lisa, it was all a ploy just to get some blue jeans?"

"Yes."

"Stealing my Game Boy?"

"Yes."

"Even the call to my hotel in Paris?"

The KGB Man sighed. "Yes. Obviously."

"But you told me to drop the case! Why would you tell me to quit if you wanted me to follow you to Moscow?"

"There are some children," said the KGB Man, "when you tell them not to do something, they want to do it even more. I thought you seemed one of these children."

"That sounds like something this guy I know, Craig, would say, only he speaks in better English."

The KGB Man shrugged. "Well, I am Russian."

"I find this all hard to believe."

"And yet this is totally real," said the KGB Man. "You see? I am the one who is moving the pieces."

"Seems like a whole lot of trouble to go through for some jeans."

"What do people want more than anything else?" said the KGB Man. "They want what they cannot have."

I looked down at my jeans.

They were perfectly faded.

And there was no way my mom was going to buy me a new pair.

But I had a duty to the Queen.

"OK," I said.

"Excellent," said the KGB Man.

I handed over my jeans.

The KGB Man handed over the loot.

CHAPTER 16

JEAN CRIME

"Can I at least have another pair of pants?" I asked. "You know, for the road?"

"*Nyet,*" said the KGB Man.

"What does that mean?"

"No."

It was a cold walk through Moscow.
And a very long flight.

But the Queen of England got her spoon back.

France got the Mona Lisa.

And I got home. It was Saturday morning.

My mom was happy to see me. She had missed me very much, plus the rabbits' litter box needed to be emptied.

There was a package for me on the kitchen counter.

It was from the Queen of England.

Dear Agent Mac,
Enclosed you will find a note for your teacher, explaining your absence, as well as a reward to thank you for your service to me, the Queen of England. Best wishes from the entire royal family, including Freddie, whose habit of licking seems to have worsened while he was under your care.

My Majesty,

The Queen of England

There was an envelope addressed to my teacher, and a box wrapped in purple paper and tied with a gold bow.

The tag said, "Something delicious from Britain!"

I eagerly unwrapped the gift.

It was a tin covered with fancy royal decorations.

I opened the tin.

Biscuits.

I tried one, to see if these were any better than the last batch.

They weren't.

This was not the reward I had been hoping for.

To be honest, I had been expecting to get knighted.

But I wasn't a knight.

I was a secret agent.

And being a secret agent is not easy.

I swallowed the biscuit.

Then I leaned back in my chair and turned on my Game Boy.

"No!" I said.

"No!" I said again.

I was looking at the high-score screen.

It was going to take me forever to beat that.

(The KGB is only three letters. Great name.)

Before I could even get past level one, the phone rang.

It was Derek Lafoy, inviting me to his birthday party!

Just kidding.

That would have been a nice ending, but remember, this story is real.

It was the Queen of England.

"Hullo," said the Queen. "Don't even bother thanking me for the biscuits. There isn't any time! Mac, I need another favor."

I smiled.

OK.

THE

END

Mac Barnett is a *New York Times* bestselling author of children's books and a former █████. His books have received awards such as the Caldecott Honor, the E. B. White Read Aloud Award, and the Boston Globe-Horn Book Award. His secret agent work has received awards such as the Medal of █████, the Cross of █████, and the Royal Order of █████ █████ the Third. His favorite color is █████. His favorite food is █████. He lives in Oakland, California. (That's true. You can look it up.)

Mike Lowery used to get in trouble for doodling in his books, and now he's doing it for a living. His drawings have been seen in dozens of books for kids and adults, and on everything from greeting cards to food trucks. He also likes to collect weird little bits of knowledge and recently collected them in his book, *Random Illustrated Facts*. Mike lives in Atlanta, Georgia, with a little German lady and two genius kids.

LOOK OUT FOR THE NEXT

MAC B. KID SPY

ADVENTURE!

THE IMPOSSIBLE CRIME

Praise For MAC UNDERCOVER

Funny as a crumpet. (But truly, secretly a hundred times smarter.)

— **JON SCIESZKA,**
author of *The Stinky Cheese Man and Other Fairly Stupid Tales*

Barnett royally nails it.

— **ABBY HANLON,**
author of *Dory Fantasmagory*